POCKET PUB WALKS

Surrey

David Weller

COUNTRYSIDE BOOKS
NEWBURY BERKSHIRE

First published 2007
© David Weller, 2007

COUNTRYSIDE BOOKS
3 Catherine Road
Newbury, Berkshire

To view our complete range of books,
please visit us at
www.countrysidebooks.co.uk

ISBN 978 1 84674 023 7

Maps and photographs by the author
Cover picture of Marden Park supplied by Derek Forss

*To my wife Marilyn
for her invaluable help and support*

Designed by Peter Davies, Nautilus Design
Produced through MRM Associates Ltd, Reading
Printed by Borcombe SP Ltd., Romsey

Contents

POCKET PUB WALKS

④ Englefield Green

WEYBRIDGE

③ Chobham

⑩ Downside   ⑭ Warlingham
⑫ Mickleham

⑥ Cartbridge

Staffhurst
GUILDFORD   *DORKING*   *REIGATE*   ⑮ Wood

⑤ Artington

⑨ Sutton Abinger   ⑬ Outwood

FARNHAM

① Tilford   ⑧ Blackheath

⑪ Capel

⑦ Cranleigh

② Hindhead

Area map showing location of the walks

Introduction

What a great idea it is to combine a lovely walk in the Surrey countryside with a good pub lunch, after all, the county is such a wonderfully diverse place and a great pleasure to explore. Majestic native woodland, scenic towpaths where colourful narrow boats negotiate the locks, wildflower meadows where butterflies skip from flower to flower in their search for ever more nectar, rose-bedecked cottages overlooking pretty village greens and exhilarating panoramic views, all combining to make it a delight for those on a leisurely walk.

I have not designed these circuits to test your stamina, nor your map reading expertise, but solely to help you enjoy walking the lovely paths and tracks through Surrey's magnificent countryside. They are all based on good pubs where you can immerse yourself in the convivial atmosphere of the bar, or the cheerful laughter from the garden on a summer's day, while during winter, draw your chair closer to the inglenook and warm yourself in front of the glowing embers of an open fire. Whatever the season, let's face it, there's nothing better than that contented feeling one has after a good walk as you sink into a comfortable chair and enjoy a fine meal washed down with a real ale.

Not all the pubs have parking facilities, but for those that do, the majority of landlords have agreed to let patrons use them whilst on the walk, but please ask first. For those not wishing to use the pub car parks, I have in each case suggested the use of nearby alternative parking. My sketch maps are drawn to scale and they will aid you around the circuit but are no substitute for the Ordnance Survey map I have recommended at the beginning of each walk, which gives a better overview of the surrounding area. To make following my sketch maps easier, the numbered paragraphs in my text correspond to those on each map.

Now armed with this little book, put your walking shoes on and explore all that Surrey can offer, for there is much of interest to see while walking the paths, cart tracks and byways that my routes follow.

Happy walking!

Publisher's Note

We hope that you obtain considerable enjoyment from this book; great care has been taken in its preparation. However, changes of landlord and actual closures are sadly not uncommon. Likewise, although at the time of publication all routes followed public rights of way or permitted paths, diversion orders can be made and permissions withdrawn.

We cannot, of course, be held responsible for such diversion orders and any inaccuracies in the text which result from these or any other changes to the routes nor any damage which might result from walkers trespassing on private property. We are anxious though that all details covering the walks and pubs are kept up to date and would therefore welcome information from readers which would be relevant to future editions.

The simple sketch maps that accompany the walks in this book are based on notes made by the author whilst checking out the routes on the ground. However, for the benefit of a proper map, we do recommend that you purchase the relevant Ordnance Survey sheet covering your walk. The Ordnance Survey maps are widely available, especially through booksellers and local newsagents.

1 Tilford

The Barley Mow

Tilford village green must be one of the prettiest in the south-east of England. This great walk begins at the green and soon follows a pleasant track that brings us to the scenic waters of Stockbridge Pond where the surrounding woodland is

Distance – 4¼ miles.

OS Landranger 186 Aldershot & Guildford, Camberley & Haslemere. GR 874434.

An easy walk over fairly level terrain.

Starting point Tilford village green. Additional parking at point 2.

How to get there *From the A3 south of Guildford, turn west at the Milford junction on the B3001. Some 1½ miles after passing through Elstead, turn left as signposted to reach Tilford. Cross the bridge and park alongside the river.*

mirrored in its still waters. Continuing through majestic stands of pine, the way reaches the open heath of Hankley Common below Yagden Hill where there are spectacular views over the area. After following a sandy track across Hankley golf course, the circuit joins with a quiet road for a short distance before beginning to head back along level tracks through Tilford Common. Near the end of the route the way passes through a bluebell wood where the bank of the river Wey is followed the short distance back to Tilford.

THE PUB

The **Barley Mow** is formed out of two old cottages, one of which is 400 years old which goes some way to explain the higgledy-piggledy interior with different floor levels that impart a homely character. I visited on a summer's lunchtime and chose to sit in the large riverside garden where the rural views are truly magnificent. The menu includes a selection of ploughman's, baked potatoes and toasted sandwiches with a daily special on the blackboard. The ales from the pumps include Young's, Courage Best, Abbot Ale and London Pride.

Tilford Walk 1

Opening times: 11 am to 3 pm and 6 pm to 11 pm weekdays and 11 am to 11 pm on Saturday and 12 noon to 11 pm on Sunday.
☎ *01252 792205*

1 With your back to the **Barley Mow**, walk along the left edge of the green to reach a road junction by **All Saints Infants School**. Press on ahead along a bridleway that continues along the left side of the road.

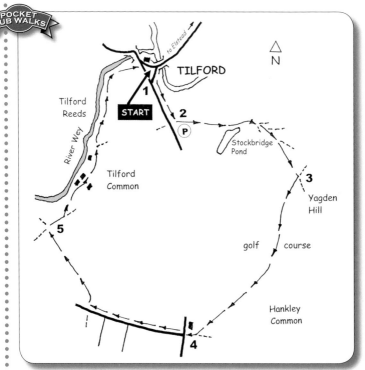

The 13th-century bridge over the river Wey beside Tilford Green.

2 At a crossing track with a parking area ahead of you, turn left along the track and remain on it until it meets with a vehicle barrier by the end of **Stockbridge Pond**. The path continues past the vehicle barrier and 30 yards later divides into three where you should take the central narrowest path that rises between banks to reach an open grassy area. Now press on ahead and ignore a wide track forking to the left. In 90 yards when the path forks, keep to the right fork and soon your way leaves the trees behind and begins to cross open heath where you will see **Yagden Hill** ahead of you.

3 At a sandy crossing track, turn right towards **Hankley golf course** in the distance. Now remain on this path for 1 mile as it leads you through the middle of the course; please take note of the signs regarding flying golf balls. As the path leaves the course it narrows and continues down a dip through trees to meet a track. Go right here to meet with a road in 35 yards beside **Gorse Cottage**.

4 Cross the road and continue along **Grange Road** opposite. Pass by the end of **Eglinton Road** and the almost hidden **Winchester Road**. About 40 yards after passing a very large garden with a low wall surmounted by railings, turn right on a signed bridleway that skirts a large plant nursery and ends at a junction of tracks by the end of the growing grounds.

5 Turn right here and, after 120 yards, turn left over a stile and continue on a fenced path. At a driveway press on ahead and pass two houses. Just 10 yards after the entrance to a third house, fork left on a narrower path between trees and go through a gate. Remain on this path as it leads you through pretty woodland and along the bank of the **river Wey** before finally ending at a road beside the village green where you will see the **Barley Mow** beyond.

Places of interest nearby

The **Rural Life Centre** at Reeds Road, Tilford, is a museum of village life recording the past 250 years. Set in 10 acres of woodland, there are displays of village crafts, and for the young, a historic village playground. With a narrow-gauge railway and 100 acres of arboretum, it is a splendid place to visit. Open April to October Wednesday to Sunday between 10 am and 5 pm; November to March Wednesday and Sunday only, 11 am to 4 pm.
☎ *01252 795571*

2 Hindhead

The Devil's Punchbowl Hotel

Despite its ominous name, the Devil's Punchbowl is Surrey's premier beauty spot and this circuit is surely the best the county can offer. Beginning at the rim of the punchbowl, we follow a wonderful woodland track down to the isolated vale of Highcomb Bottom which was once the home of 'broom squires'. The area is a pleasure to explore and here we cross a small stream and pass by an isolated youth hostel before following a wonderful track with magnificent views that is shared by a section of the Greensand Way long-distance path. On our return, the path leads us through a pretty dell where we re-cross the stream and pass by 15th-century Ridgeway Farm. Soon the circuit follows a bridleway that climbs easily through stands of pine and returns us to the Punchbowl and the end of this excellent walk.

THE PUB

The **Devil's Punchbowl Hotel** started life as a temperance hotel but that has all been swept away many years ago and there is no sign of any sort of restraint nowadays, especially on the food served in the bar and restaurant. The mouth-watering selection begins with tapas that include tomato and mozzarella salad and chilli prawn bruschetta, while more substantial dishes include spit roast chicken in a barbeque sauce, gammon hock in a honey and mustard sauce and shank of lamb cooked in red wine and rosemary – all at very reasonable prices. From the pumps come bitters that include Tetley, Bass and Wadworth 6X.

Opening times: The bar is open from 11 am to 11 pm each day (Sunday 12 noon to 10.30 pm) although tea and coffee is served from 8 am (Sunday from 10.30 am). Restaurant food is served from 12 noon until 9.30 pm and booking is advisable.

☎ *01428 606565*

Distance – 5¼ miles.

OS Landranger 186 Aldershot & Guildford, Camberley & Haslemere. GR 891358.

An energetic walk although not too taxing.

Starting point National Trust pay and display car park by the Devil's Punchbowl Café.

How to get there On the A3 just ¼ mile north of the main traffic lights in Hindhead you will find the Devil's Punchbowl Hotel with the National Trust car park opposite.

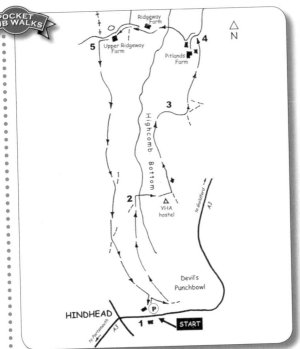

1 From the **Devil's Punchbowl National Trust car park**, cross a grassy picnic area to reach a viewpoint that offers extensive views over the punchbowl. Follow a wide path rightwards alongside the rim to reach a kissing gate and 5 yards later turn left on a wonderful woodland path. Now ignore side paths for ¾ mile as the magnificent path descends into **Highcomb Bottom**.

2 Pass through a second kissing gate and keep ahead to reach field gates on either side of the track and a line of old beech trees, now all joined together. After 50 yards turn right through a kissing gate and follow a narrower path through a dell where you

The fantastic panorama from the viewpoint.

cross a stream. Climb out of the dell on a broad track and pass to the left of a remote youth hostel half hidden behind a hedgerow. With a metalled lane ahead of you, turn left through a gate and continue on a downhill track passing by **Gnome Cottage**, surely the most remote in Surrey. Soon cross a cattle grid and now remain on this wonderful track as it leads you through beautiful scenery for just over ½ mile.

3 After going round a right-hand bend soon followed by a left bend, pass a field gate on either side of the track to reach a fork.

Follow the left fork and in 80 yards ignore a track on your right and press on ahead to cross a cattle grid.

4 At a junction with a small tarmac lane, turn left along the lane for 45 yards before forking right on a downhill path beside a cottage. Soon cross a stream in this narrow valley and go diagonally left up a fairly steep, deeply eroded track to meet with **Ridgeway Farm**, which has its beginnings back in the 15th century. Continue ahead along a tarmac lane and ignore a lane to your right. Press on along **Hyde Lane** and soon pass idyllic **Upper Ridgeway Farm** and its attractive duck pond.

5 The lane soon goes down a dip and here look out for a byway on your right. Opposite this to your left is a less easily spotted bridleway which you should now follow. After passing between banks go through a gate and press on ahead on the wide bridleway under power cables for 1¼ miles. When the rim of the punchbowl is reached go on ahead as the path follows the escarpment. Pass through a gate and under a vehicle height barrier and 80 yards later fork left along a broad track with gardens on your right. When the viewpoint is met, turn right and a few yards later the end of this splendid circuit is reached.

Places of interest nearby

Set in lovely countryside, **Grayshott Pottery** in School Road, Grayshott just south-west of Hindhead is open each day. It has a spacious gift shop that offers a wide range of gifts from Dartington crystal, jewellery, stationery, to cushions, candles and more. There is a café bistro and patio garden, where you can enjoy tea, coffee, soft drinks, cakes, lunches, wines and beers. Take the A3 south for ⅓ mile and then turn west for 1 mile on the B3002.
☎ 01428 604404

3 Chobham

The Sun Inn

Chobham is tucked into the far north-western part of Surrey and the village remains quite isolated. This lovely circuit begins in the heart of the village and it will come as some surprise that within just a few yards of leaving the High Street you are immersed in the wonderful wildflower meadows of Sow Moor, the home to myriads of butterflies during summer. For almost half the route we follow the lush banks of the Mill Bourne on a path that leads us to Emmett's Mill, which now serves as a fine residence. From here the way continues across open fields and paddocks before joining with a pleasant tree-lined lane that brings us to a pretty bridleway. After following this through woodland we all too soon find ourselves back in the heart of the village where this great walk ends.

Distance - 3¾ miles.

OS Landranger 176 West London area. GR *pub* 974617, *free car park* 974618.

An easy walk through level countryside.

Starting point The Sun Inn or at point 2.

How to get there Chobham can be reached via Junction 11 of the M25. Follow the A320 south before heading south-west on the A319 signed to Chobham. The Sun Inn is in the centre of the High Street and patrons may leave their cars there (please ask first). There is alternative parking at point 2.

THE PUB The **Sun Inn** is unique as far as I know as it was purchased by 23 enthusiastic locals who outbid a large coffee house chain in order to keep the only remaining pub in the High Street as their 'local'. Were their efforts worthwhile? Of course they were, for the visitor is treated to an abundance of old oak beams decorated with trailing hops, open fireplaces and a friendly welcome. The simple lunchtime bar menu offers sandwiches, baguettes and jacket potatoes, all with a good selection of fillings while the à la carte menu in the restaurant gives a wider selection, although food is not available on Mondays. The large selection of beers includes Courage Best, London Pride and Hogs Back TEA.

Opening times: 11.30 am to 3 pm and 5.30 pm to 11 pm each day (Sundays 12 noon to 3 pm and 6 pm to 10.30 pm). Booking for cooked meals is recommended.
☎ *01276 857112*

Chobham Walk 3

1 With the **Sun Inn** at your back, turn left along the **High Street** and pass St Lawrence's church. Keep ahead at a mini roundabout and pass **Cannon Corner** where a Russian 24-pounder commemorates a visit made by Queen Victoria in 1853 when she reviewed her troops on Chobham Common. Turn right into the entrance drive of the free car park.

2 Just 20 yards from the car park entrance take the fenced footpath signed '**Eve's Path**' and follow it alongside the car park to reach a meadow. Bear left here to soon reach the **Mill Bourne** and now go right on a well-trodden path as it shadows the stream and passes through several wildflower meadows. Ignore side paths and remain close to the bank of the stream until the path finally meets with a metal stile. Cross this and go ahead on a wide path signed to **Emmett's Mill**.

3 Follow the path to reach a stile at a field edge. Cross this and continue ahead and after 80 yards pass through a hedgerow. Now follow the field edge as it bears off rightwards alongside the **Mill Bourne**. At the end of the field press on along a narrow path by the stream and cross two small wooden bridges to reach a road.

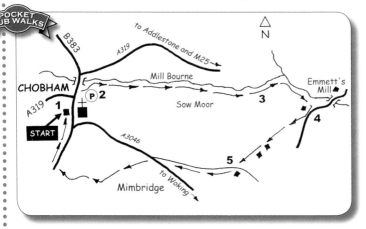

4 Turn right along the road and pass the entrance gates to **Fairbourne Manor**. Now look out for a half-hidden kissing gate on your right at the beginning of a paddock. Pass through this and follow the well-signed footpath through a series of paddocks and to the rear of several gardens. Keep ahead through another paddock to reach a quiet road by **Chobham Farm**.

Cannon Corner.

5 Turn right here along this pleasant road where a few houses hide among the trees. Follow it left to meet **Station Road** and cross to a bridleway that begins at a private drive opposite. The Victorians optimistically named this road in eager anticipation of the railway coming to Chobham – it didn't! Follow the bridleway through woodland and after crossing a planked bridge turn right along a concrete drive. The drive ends beside a house that displays the changing architecture of time admirably; the rear is plainly Tudor while the frontage is Georgian. Turn right to soon meet with a mini roundabout where you should go ahead and within yards rejoin the **Sun Inn** and the end of this good walk.

Places of interest nearby

Chobham Museum opposite Cannon Corner in point 1 of the walk is a small village museum staffed by volunteers. The exhibits include 200 old photographs of the village. Open March to October 11 am to 4 pm on Wednesdays and weekends; November to February 11.30 am to 3.30 pm weekends only.
☎ *01276 858322*

4 Englefield Green

The Barley Mow

Even though the large towns of Egham and Staines are in close proximity, Englefield Green remains, surprisingly, a quintessential Surrey village. Clustered around the southern edge of the large green are pretty cottages and a fine public house where our circuit begins. This enjoyable route passes the Commonwealth Air Forces Memorial on top of Cooper's Hill, a fascinating and quite unique monument. Soon the way descends through oak woodland and reaches Runnymede's historic water meadows where we join the bank of the river Thames. A pleasant stroll along the water's edge takes us through the Runnymede Pleasure Grounds where a café offering hot and cold drinks and snacks can be found. Leaving the river, the circuit makes its way back through water meadows awash with wildflowers before tackling the none-too-difficult ascent back to Englefield Green.

THE PUB

The **Barley Mow** has links to what is believed to have been the last duel fought in Britain, strangely enough between two Frenchmen. The loser was carried to the pub where he died a few hours later. Putting those dark events to the back of your mind, you will enjoy the light and uncluttered convivial interior as well as the sunny patio and large garden where you can relax and treat yourself to the splendid dishes offered on the keenly priced menu. Try the Barley Mow Burger, it's enormous! The beers from the pumps include London Pride, Adnams Broadside, Old Speckled Hen and Wadworth 6X.

Opening times: 11.30 am to 11.30 pm each day; Sunday 12 noon to 10.30 pm. Booking a table for cooked meals is essential during winter when the garden is out of use.
☎ *01784 431857*

1 With your back to the **Barley Mow**, walk across the green and pass to the right of the cricket pitch. When nearing the A328,

Distance – 4 miles.

OS Landranger 176 West London area. GR 992774.

The circuit ends with a fairly easy ascent of 270 feet that will not trouble the average person.

Starting point The Barley Mow beside the green.

How to get there *Englefield Green is on the A328, 1 mile south-west of Egham. When travelling along the A30 turn onto the A328 opposite the Royal Holloway College and after 1 mile the green will be seen on your left. Parking is at the roadside.*

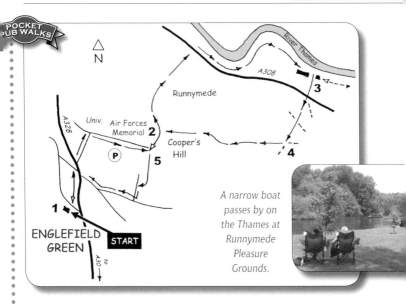

A narrow boat passes by on the Thames at Runnymede Pleasure Grounds.

pass a mini roundabout by **Middle Hill** and continue on for 50 yards before turning right alongside a road signed to the Air Forces Memorial. At a T-junction with **Cooper's Hill Lane**, turn right and soon after passing the memorial car park, the gates of the distinctive monument are reached. The way passes the gates and continues along the lane as it bends leftwards and passes **Kingswood Hall** of the Royal Holloway College.

2 When the tarmac surface ends in 70 yards, turn left through a kissing gate and follow a stepped path that descends through the magnificent woodland of **Cooper's Hill**. Stay on the main path and when it reaches Runnymede's famous water meadows below, press on ahead to meet with the A308 main road. Cross the road and go right on a grassy path that follows the bank of the **river Thames**. Soon you will pass along the edge of the manicured **Runnymede Pleasure Grounds** where over to your right is a café serving light refreshments.

Surrey

3 Immediately after passing a commercial building, turn right on a path between it and **Thames Cottage** although you may if you wish extend the route by 1 mile by continuing along the river bank to **Bell Weir Lock** before returning. Continue alongside the commercial building and re-cross the A308. Ignore a grassy path that goes diagonally half left and follow a grassy path straight ahead. After 200 yards, press on alongside a hedgerow and when this begins to veer off to the right, a crossing path is met.

4 Now turn right and follow the indistinct path to reach a kissing gate under an oak tree at the side of a meadow. Go through this and continue up a rise to reach another kissing gate at the far side where you join a track. Turn right along the rising track which climbs steadily and brings you back to **Kingswood Hall** of the Royal Holloway College.

5 Immediately after passing the buildings and as the road bends to the right, bear left on a fenced path and follow this to reach a tree-lined residential road. Continue left along the pavement until this short residential road ends at a T-junction. Turn right alongside the road and at **Middle Hill** press on ahead to soon rejoin the A328 at a mini roundabout and the green. Turn left along the green to meet with the **Barley Mow** and the end of this interesting circuit.

Places of interest nearby

The **Commonwealth Air Forces Memorial** is passed near the beginning of the route. It commemorates the 20,401 airmen and women who have no known grave and, quite appropriately, resembles an airfield control tower. Visitors may climb the spiral stairs to the rooftop viewing platform that offers magnificent views. Open each day during daylight hours. Unfortunately dogs are not allowed in the grounds.

5 Artington

Ye Olde Ship Inn

Artington is a southerly suburb of Guildford set above the river Wey and beside the old Pilgrim's Way path. This great circuit first heads off westerly and follows a pleasant track along the foot of the Hog's Back where splendid views over fields can be enjoyed. As the way turns and heads back towards Guildford, it continues through the grounds of Loseley House and passes a serene lake where picnic tables entice you to stay awhile and admire its beauty. After crossing level fields, the route meets with the river Wey by St Catherine's Lock where colourful pleasure boats negotiate the gates on their way to and from Godalming. A pleasant stroll along the river bank ensues, which brings us back to Artington and the end of this varied and most enjoyable walk.

THE PUB **Ye Olde Ship Inn** boasts that it is the oldest pub in Guildford and is proud of the fact that it has no music or fruit machines – just good old-fashioned hospitality; there is even a sign that asks patrons to switch off their mobile phones – bliss! The interior is a riot of oak beams, stone walls and open fireplaces, which give the three bar areas a great atmosphere. There is a good selection of home-cooked food on the menu from which I chose a mature cheddar cheese ploughman's piled high with salad and pickles and supplied with a warm baguette while my wife fought her way through a baked potato overflowing with prawns in Marie Rose sauce. Beers from the pump include Greene King ales, Guinness, Abbot Ale and Old Speckled Hen.

Opening times: 11 am to 3 pm and 5 pm to 11 pm each day; Sunday 10.30 pm closing.
☎ *01483 575731*

Distance – 4¼ miles.

OS Landranger 186 Aldershot & Guildford, Camberley & Haslemere. GR pub 994483, *Ferry Lane* 994482.

An easy walk through open countryside with just one very short but stiff hill.

Starting point Cars may be left in Ye Olde Ship Inn car park if you are a patron (please ask first) or alternatively there is limited parking in Ferry Lane a few yards south of the pub.

How to get there Artington is on the A3100 Portsmouth Road, 1 mile south of Guildford town centre. Ye Olde Ship Inn is at the roadside.

POCKET
PUB WALKS

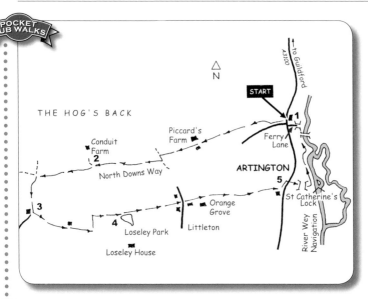

THE HOG'S BACK

Conduit
Farm
2

North Downs Way

Piccard's
Farm

START

1

Ferry
Lane

ARTINGTON

5

St Catherine's
Lock

3

4

Orange
Grove

Loseley Park

Littleton

River Wey
Navigation

Loseley House

△
N

to Guildford
A3100

1. From either the **Ye Olde Ship Inn** or **Ferry Lane** cross the A3100 and continue along **Sandy Lane** opposite the pub. After 200 yards turn right on a track signed as the **North Downs Way** and almost immediately you are immersed into scenic countryside. Go straight on at all times and pass the buildings of **Piccard's Farm** where you continue ahead along the farm lane. Keep to the lane when it turns sharply left but after 90 yards, turn right along the signed **North Downs Way** as it continues along a track through woodland.

2. When the track goes downhill and turns sharply right towards **Conduit Farm**, the route forks left and maintains the original direction on a narrow sandy path that begins to rise between banks. Pass the crest of the rise and 70 yards later, at a junction of bridleways, you should turn left down the hill. Remain on this bridleway until the entrance gate of a house named **Little Polsted** is reached.

The expansive view towards the Hog's Back.

3 Now turn left along a cart track and pass a house in ½ mile. Continue through a gateway and press on along the drive to reach a second gateway in 280 yards. Here turn left over a stile and follow a narrow path that skirts the grounds of **Loseley House**. Soon after crossing two stiles in quick succession, go right over a stile to reach a scenic lake where you may like to take advantage of the picnic tables on the bank.

4 The way continues along the bank where all too soon you leave the water's edge and cross a stile and continue on a path that crosses the centre of two fields before passing between houses to meet with a lane in the hamlet of **Littleton**. Go ahead here on a short lane that ends at the gates of a large house named **Orange Grove**. Maintain direction now along a grassy path that soon follows the boundary of a police dog training school. Eventually the path ends at a road where you should continue ahead to reach the A3100 main road.

5 Turn left along the pavement alongside the A3100 for 60 yards before turning right across the road and continuing along a track to the left of a bus stop. Press on under a railway bridge to soon reach **St Catherine's Lock** on the river Wey Navigation. Turn left along the towpath and finally pass under the sand cliffs of **St Catherine's**. Soon after going under a footbridge seek out a path to your left beside a spring that flows into the river. Turn left here and after a short climb up **Ferry Lane** the A3100 is rejoined where a few yards to your right you will meet **Ye Olde Ship Inn** and the end of this great walk.

Places of interest nearby

Dapdune Wharf, in Guildford, was once a boat-building yard servicing the Wey Navigation. Now a museum containing a boat shed, forge and a hand-operated crane, it tells the story of those who lived and worked on the waterway. Among the attractions are regular boat trips on the restored barge *Reliance*.
☎ *01483 561389*

The New Inn

This great little circuit begins by following the towpath of the river Wey Navigation where colourful narrow boats cruise the still waters that reflect the magnificent scenery of these parts. After passing Worsfold Gates – a lock with a rise in water level of only a few inches – the walk continues along the appealing towpath and crosses the meandering river Wey to reach Triggs Lock, a fascinating place to stop and watch narrow boats negotiate the gates. With Send Grove's water meadows away to our left and the tower of the parish church in the distance, we take our leave of the canal and soon follow a quiet lane that brings us to a pleasurable field path bordered on one side by a hedgerow brimming with wildlife and with open views on the other and all too soon we find ourselves back at Cartbridge.

Distance – 2½ miles.

OS Landranger 186 Aldershot & Guildford, Camberley & Haslemere. GR 017559.

An easy level walk.

Starting point The New Inn in Potters Lane, but please ask first if leaving your car here. Plenty of roadside parking along Potters Lane.

How to get there Potters Lane is off the A247 at Cartbridge ⅓ mile south of Old Woking; turn off the A3 near Ripley. When approaching from the A3, the New Inn and Potters Lane will be met on your left just before the bridge over the canal.

THE PUB The **New Inn** is early Victorian and a part of it once served as a mortuary which gives rise to the belief by some locals that the saying 'to have a stiff drink' emanates from here. Well, whether it did or didn't, I am not convinced, but one thing I am sure of is that you will not be disappointed by a visit. The reasonably priced food is excellent and ranges from toasties, jacket potatoes, baguettes and steak dishes. Relax in the canal-side garden during the summer and watch the narrow boats pass by as you indulge yourself. The beers include Greene King Abbot Ale, Fuller's London Pride, Adnam's Bitter and Ringwood Best Bitter.

Opening times: 11 am to 11 pm each day (Sunday 12 noon to 10.30 pm). Food is served throughout the day and booking is not required.
☎ *01483 762736*

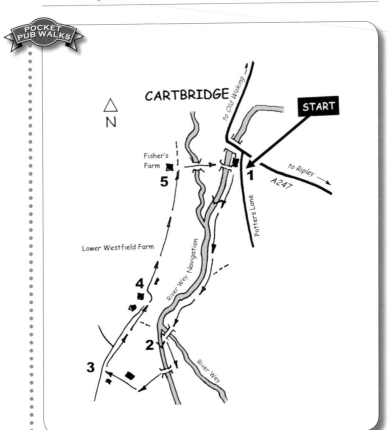

CARTBRIDGE

START

to Old Woking

Fisher's Farm

5

to Ripley

A247

Potters Lane

Lower Westfield Farm

River Wey Navigation

4

2

3

River Wey

1

△ N

1 Walk back to the A247, turn left and pass the front of the **New Inn** before turning left again along a gravel lane immediately after the pub. Now continue alongside the **river Wey Navigation** on the towpath where you pass the rear of houses and soon reach **Worsfold Gates**, the canal's lowest rise. The route continues along the canal and crosses a bridge over the **river Wey** when it enters the canal from the left.

2 Pass by **Triggs Lock** and after 300 yards, turn right over a small bridge. Now follow a narrow path between two fields to reach a farm track. Turn right here and pass the buildings of **Wareham's Farm**, some now converted into a fine large house. Press on along the drive to meet with a country lane.

3 Turn right along the lane and soon ignore **Robin Hood Lane** on your left. Press on ahead along **Runtley Wood Lane** to meet with a junction of paths in front of a bungalow. Here ignore a

Narrow boats negotiating Triggs Lock.

footpath on your right beside a vehicle barrier, but in a further 10 yards cross a stile on your right. Follow the path leftwards to soon reach the gates to beautiful **Runtley Wood Farmhouse**. Turn right now along the drive and look out for a signed concrete path on your right that skirts a garden. Soon follow the signed path rightwards and pass a stable block.

4 The path now continues alongside a hedgerow that must supply the local wildlife with nuts, fruit and berries for most of the year – hazelnuts, haws, blackberries, acorns and sloes aplenty. Remain on the path now until it finally meets a stile beside the gateway to **Fisher's Farm.**

5 Cross the stile and turn right along a concrete drive where you soon cross the **river Wey**. Ignore a footpath to your left and press on to meet a bend in the drive. Bear right here to meet and cross a footbridge over the **Wey Navigation**. Now it is only a few yards leftwards along the towpath before you rejoin the **New Inn** and the end of this good short walk.

Places of interest nearby

Clandon Park, three miles north-east of Guildford, on the A247 is one of the country's most complete Palladian mansions and contains superb 17th-century furniture and tapestries. Outside in the lovely grounds are formal gardens, a grotto and a unique carved wood Maori meeting house. Open 12 noon until 5 pm from March to October on Tuesdays, Wednesdays, Thursdays and Sundays.
☎ *01483 222482*

7 Cranleigh

The White Hart

Cranleigh is Surrey's largest village and the locals are justly proud of it. This panhandle walk begins from near where the railway station once stood, but that sadly was lost to the village during the infamous Beeching cuts of 1965. Since then the track has been transformed; nowadays it leads a much quieter life and the old track bed forms a part of the Downs Link long-distance footpath and the days when steam trains rattled through here spewing out their smoke and hot cinders have long been forgotten. This route takes in almost 2 miles of the track bed, which has become an unofficial linear nature reserve. After leaving the track bed the way follows wide paths and quiet lanes as it loops through magnificent countryside before rejoining this wonderful path for the homeward journey.

THE PUB

The **White Hart** isn't the nearest pub to the beginning of the walk as that honour is held by the Three Horseshoes, a traditional village pub in the High Street serving good real ales but unfortunately not food. The quest for good food takes us 200 yards up nearby Ewhurst Road to the White Hart, once a coaching inn. The lounge area is comfortable with an open fireplace and here you can choose from the simple bar menu that ranges from jacket potatoes, burgers, ploughman's and a range of other dishes from which I can heartily recommend the leek and seafood pie, it's delicious. Beers from the pumps include Courage Best and Directors. Food is served during lunchtimes and evenings.

Opening times: 11.30 am to 3 pm and 6 pm until 11 pm each day (Sunday 10.30 pm).
☎ *01483 268647*

1 From the car park continue away from the **High Street** on a path beside the leisure centre to cross a small brook and reach a

Distance – 6 miles.

OS Landranger 187 Dorking & Reigate, Crawley & Horsham. GR 058389.

An easy walk through gently undulating countryside.

Starting point Pay and display car park in Village Way by the Cranleigh Leisure Centre.

How to get there *Cranleigh is 8 miles south of Guildford on the B2128. Very limited roadside parking by the White Hart, so use the cheap pay and display car park (free on Sundays) in Village Way; turn off by the village hall in the High Street.*

Cranleigh Walk 7

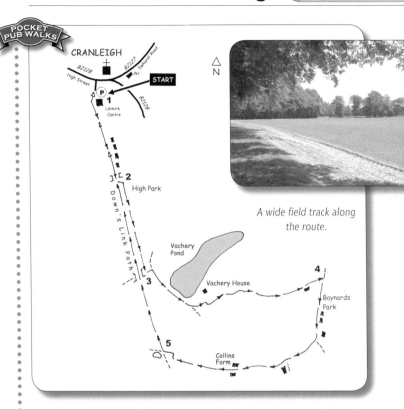

A wide field track along the route.

T-junction with a wide track. This track was once the railway line and you should now turn left along it and pass between a small car park and a sports field. A few houses will be seen through the trees on your left and 90 yards after passing the last house, look out for a wire fenced bridge parapet.

[2] Turn left here and go down steps to reach a field where you should turn right along its edge. Enter a second field and follow a cart track uphill until 30 yards before its crest; seek out a narrow path that forks slightly right. Follow this path between trees

37

The bed of the old railway makes a fine linear nature reserve.

as it shadows the old railway cutting. At the foot of a slope by a crossing track, with the railway track just 10 yards away to your right, press on ahead. The path finally ends at a stile by a track with a brick bridge on your right.

3 Turn left here along a concrete farm track until it soon ends at a T-junction with a tarmac driveway. Turn right on the bridleway along this scenic drive and ignore a left fork that leads to **Vachery House**. About 10 yards before meeting a second fork, turn left and follow the bridleway along a cart track and pass between

buildings. After passing entrance gates, follow the bridleway left as it continues along the left-hand boundary of a large field. Press on as it follows the left side of a second field but, when the well-worn track turns left at a third field, keep ahead on a narrower path that you now follow until it passes a house and ends at a tarmac driveway.

4 Turn right along the drive and pass by cottages and farm buildings. Ignore a footpath ahead at a bend and remain on the drive. At a terrace of half-tiled cottages, maintain direction ahead on a rising stony bridleway. The way meets with a concrete farm drive which you should follow between cottages and farm buildings and when this ends press on ahead along a track that soon meets with the old track bed of the defunct railway where a small private lake will be seen ahead of you.

5 Turn right here along this glorious path inhabited by wildlife; without any further instruction, stuff this little book firmly into your pocket and follow the track for 2 miles until you reach **Cranleigh** where there are coffee shops and eateries available in the **High Street** for your delight. If real ales are required then 100 yards to the right of **Village Way** you will find the **Three Horseshoes** while a short walk up **Ewhurst Road** from the mini roundabout brings you to the **White Hart** and good food.

Places of interest nearby

Winkworth Arboretum north-west of Cranleigh at Hascombe, contains over 1,000 different trees and shrubs, many of them rare. It is an ideal place for the family to visit and maybe picnic. During the spring and early summer the massed rhododendrons and azaleas give a wonderful display of colour. Open all year round from dawn to dusk.
☎ 01483 208477

The Villagers

This beautiful heathland area was visited by Queen Victoria in 1864 when she reviewed her massed volunteer troops on exercise here. During the Second World War the heath was invaded once again by troops, this time Canadian, who were stationed here – an event that ended the commoners' rights for grazing their cattle on the heath. Since then, Scots pine has grown and changed the landscape, but Blackheath still retains its splendour and is enjoyed by many ramblers. This lovely route begins by descending into a shallow valley and passing through Chilworth where the ruins of one of Britain's most important gunpowder mills are discovered in peaceful woodland. The clear water of a leat that once powered the grindstones is followed until a track is met that returns us to Blackheath. Along the route there are magnificent views over the valley.

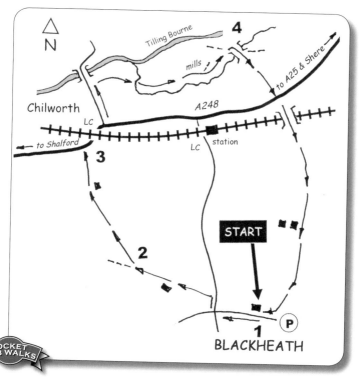

THE PUB

The **Villagers** makes a superb starting point for any walk. The village bar is basic and small but the lounge bar and restaurant area offer more comfort while the sunny woodland garden is a great place to spend a relaxing summer hour or two after the walk. The menu offers a wide choice together with a good selection of platters to share and, quite unusually, the pub boasts a seafood bar for those who enjoy a good fish meal. Not being of that ilk, I tucked into a superb caramelised red onion, tomato, artichoke and stilton tartlet with fresh tossed salad leaves at a table in the lounge. Hogs Back TEA and London Pride are among the selection of beers from the pumps.

Opening times: 12 noon to 3 pm and 6 pm to 11 pm from Monday to Thursday and from 12 noon until 11 pm Friday, Saturday and Sunday. Cooked food is available lunchtimes and evenings and booking is essential on summer weekends.
☎ *01483 893152*

Distance – 3¼ miles.

OS Landranger 186 Aldershot & Guildford, Camberley & Haslemere. GR *pub* 034462, *alternative parking* 035462.

An easy walk through undulating countryside.

Starting point The Villagers pub car park (please ask first) or alternatively Blackheath's free car park.

How to get there *Blackheath, just south-east of Guildford, is reached via the A248 at Chilworth. From Chilworth railway station turn south and go over a level crossing. Follow a narrow lane to soon reach a crossroads where you should turn left to find the pub in 200 yards; a further 100 yards brings you to the alternative parking area.*

The ruins of the old gunpowder works at Chilworth.

1 From the **Villagers** or **Blackheath car park**, walk back along the lane to the crossroads. Turn right here and after 100 yards go left on a signed bridleway between trees. At a junction of paths, press on ahead to join a driveway in 20 yards where you should bear left along it and pass a house.

2 At a junction of paths by the end of a large garden, fork right on a bridleway. The bridleway takes you downhill between banks and passes a large field where stunning panoramas across the **Tilling Bourne** valley are to be seen. The path ends at **Tangley Mere Cottage** where you should press on ahead along a track beside the house to reach the A248.

3 Cross the main road to the pavement opposite and turn right over a level crossing. Pass the end of **Old Manor Lane** and soon turn

left into **Blacksmith Lane**. Now continue along the lane until you reach a small cottage on your right called **West Lodge**. Turn right here and pass through iron gates and continue on a well-trodden path through woodland. The cottage and iron gates once formed one of the entrances to Chilworth's gunpowder factory and as you pass through the woodland you will discover many signs of the old works. Remain on the main path and ignore a left fork by a mound of earth. Continue ahead passing mill ruins beside a clear running leat to soon reach a farm lane.

4 Turn right along the lane to pass stables and reach the A248. Cross to the road opposite and after going over a railway bridge, follow the signed **Downs Link Path** as it passes to the right of a gateway of an unseen house. The path climbs easily and again there are wide reaching views over the valley. At a fork, keep right on the footpath and when by the gateway to **Lingwood House**, press on ahead along a well-trodden path that shadows a private road to your left. Soon after the path levels, ignore a left fork and continue ahead to reach a tarmac driveway. Bear right along the drive that ends at a T-junction where **Blackheath car park** will be seen on your left, while the **Villagers pub** will be found a few yards away to your right.

Places of interest nearby

Shalford Mill is an 18th-century watermill powered by the Tilling Bourne. It remained in use until 1914 after which it fell into disrepair. It is unique in that a group of well-wishers raised enough money for its restoration before presenting it to the National Trust in 1932. Sited off the A281 at Shalford, the mill is open 11 am to 5 pm on Wednesdays from end of March to end of October.
☎ *01483 561389*

The Volunteer

This must rank amongst the best walks in Surrey for the scenery it contains. Beginning in the tiny hamlet of Sutton Abinger, the route makes its way through lovely fields with far-reaching views before meeting with 16th-century Paddington Farm and passing Paddington Mill with its pretty pond. The way continues through National Trust woodland before swinging west and dropping down into the appealing village of Abinger Hammer where the Tilling Bourne cuts through its superb green. Those in need of light refreshment may like to take advantage of a great little tea shop and garden that overlooks the green a few yards off the route here. After leaving the village behind, the way climbs easily out of the valley and crosses more fields with outstanding panoramic views before rejoining Sutton Abinger.

Distance – 3¾ miles.

OS Landranger 187 Dorking & Reigate, Crawley & Horsham. GR 105459.

The circuit is through undulating countryside that is not too demanding.

Starting point The Volunteer pub in Sutton Abinger but please ask first if leaving your car there. Alternative parking at the roadside.

How to get there *Sutton Abinger is easily reached from the A25 at Abinger Hammer 5 miles west of Dorking. Turn south at Abinger Hammer's village green to meet with Sutton Abinger in 1¼ miles. The Volunteer is off Raikes Lane to your left.*

THE PUB

The **Volunteer** is a lovely pub formed from a row of cottages in the tiny hamlet of Sutton Abinger. The unpretentious interior is full of charm and the walls are decorated with ancient carpenters' tools. Outside there is a sunny patio area and a nice hillside garden. The menu offers a wide choice of reasonably priced food from which I chose a Greek salad – mixed leaves, tomato, cucumber, olives, red onion, feta cheese and enough roasted garlic to ensure that I walked alone. The notable sandwich selection includes one that contains baked cod with lime mayonnaise, lettuce and tomato served with salad and a great pile of chips! Real ales from the pumps include Sussex, Badger and Fursty Ferret.

Opening times: 11 am to 11 pm each day (Sunday 12 noon to 10.30 pm). Cooked food available lunchtimes and evenings. Booking advisable for weekend evenings.
☎ *01306 730798*

1 The route begins by going uphill on a lane beside the **Volunteer**. In 50 yards turn left on a rising bridleway and fork right when an entrance gate to a house is reached. Press on to reach a field where the way continues ahead along its right-hand edge. At a corner of the field, ignore a footpath on your right and bear off left for 30 yards before bearing right along the signed bridleway. In 120 yards, ignore a footpath signed to your left and press on ahead as the bridleway goes downhill between fields and hedgerows.

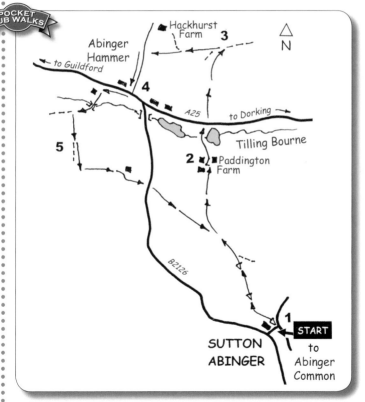

Great views are a feature of this circuit.

2 The bridleway brings you to **Paddington Farm** where you should zigzag left and right between the farm buildings. The farmhouse is early 16th-century and the great barn has recently been restored, but I wonder if its modern counterpart will last as long. Continue along the farm drive and pass between **Paddington Mill** – now a house – and the scenic millpond to soon reach the A25. Cross the road and continue ahead up a gully to reach a field gate. Pass through and continue ahead at a second gate to enter woodland.

3 At a T-junction in 60 yards turn left and remain on the wide track ignoring a narrow path to your left. After going downhill, the track turns sharply right and here you should press on ahead through a gate and follow a path along the left side of a field. Pass through a second gate to reach a quiet lane which you should follow leftwards until it ends in **Abinger Hammer**.

4 If you wish to explore the village green, it is to your left, as is the splendid **Abinger Hammer tearoom and garden**. Our way continues rightwards along the pavement by the A25 where we immediately pass the **Abinger Arms**. After passing an unusual seat, turn left on a signed bridleway along a track and shortly pass a group of houses. Beyond the **Tilling Bourne**, the entrance gate to **Brook Cottage** is met and here you should turn left on a bridleway that continues up a rise between banks that show plenty of evidence of our nocturnal wildlife.

5 Look out for a stile and a signed path on your left that brings you to a field. Turn right along the field edge and just before the crest of the hill is met, turn left on a signed path across the centre of the field. Cross a stile at the far side and go right on a narrow path that skirts a garden and goes downhill to reach a road. Cross a stile opposite and continue on a rising path. Ignore a stile on your right that invites you to explore **Oxmoor Copse** and press on ahead. The way now follows a line of power cables across two fields until it rejoins the outward path where you should retrace your steps back to **Sutton Abinger** and the end of this great circuit.

Places of interest nearby

Goddards, one mile east of Sutton Abinger, is regarded as one of Edwin Lutyens' most important houses. Designed by him in 1898, it is built in the traditional Surrey style with a garden by his great collaborator, Gertrude Jekyll. It was intended originally as 'a home of rest to which ladies of small means might repair for a holiday'. Part of the ground floor and garden is open by appointment on Wednesday afternoons between Easter and October. Must be pre-booked.
☎ *(weekdays) 01306 730871*

The Cricketers

Downside is one of those Surrey hamlets seemingly known only to locals and its prettiness will surprise those who have not visited before. The well-spaced houses spread around the tidy village green are complemented by the village hall, club, chapel and the Cricketers public house. The

Downside Walk 10

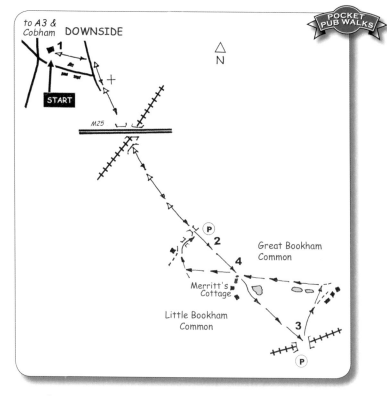

route begins by crossing the large green to reach a lane that serves no more than a couple of farms. The lane leads us to the splendour of Great Bookham Common where the native woodland is a treat for those with an interest in nature – bring your binoculars. Easily-followed tracks lead you around the forest where you have every chance of spotting woodpeckers while during spring and early summer many butterflies visit the wayside flowers. The route passes a couple of woodland pools – home to water birds and dragonflies – before rejoining the lane that returns us to Downside.

THE PUB

The **Cricketers** dates back to the 16th century although it wasn't until the mid 19th century that it became a pub. The interior exudes plenty of character with oak-beamed ceilings, crooked walls and open fireplaces while the garden overlooks the village green. The bar menu offers plenty of choice at reasonable prices; I chose a superb avocado, tomato and mozzarella salad while others at the table enjoyed smoked salmon and king prawns with crispy salad and bread. For those who wish for something more substantial there is also an à la carte menu. The bar serves real ales that include Old Speckled Hen, Greene King IPA and Fuller's London Pride.

Opening times: 11 am to 11 pm each day (Sunday 12 noon to 10.30 pm). Bar food is served from 12 noon to 2.30 pm and from 6.30 pm until 9.30 pm.
☎ *01932 862105*

Distance - 4¾ miles.

OS Landranger 187 Dorking & Reigate, Crawley & Horsham. GR 108581.

A level route along hard-surfaced roads and tracks that offer suitable walking after heavy rain in winter.

Starting point Downside village green.

How to get there *From the A3 take the Cobham turn-off and at a roundabout in the centre of Cobham bear right into the oddly-named Between Streets. Turn south into Downside Bridge Road beside a church and after 1½ miles turn left at a crossroads and park alongside the green opposite the Cricketers.*

Wide tracks lead you through wonderful woodland.

1 With the **Cricketers** behind you, cross the green leftwards to reach a lane lined by a few well-spaced Victorian houses. Turn right along the road and pass by **Pump Cottage.** The pump itself stands between the cottage and tiny **St Michael's chapel**. Press on ahead along **Bookham Road** where you pass under the M25 and a railway bridge.

2 The lane finally crosses a small brook and turns left into **Hundred Pound Bridge** car park; 20 yards after this bridge fork right between posts on a wide bridleway and ignore a right fork in 30 yards. At a junction of tracks with a National Trust information board and **Merritt's Cottage** to your right, fork right and continue along a wide track passing **Merritt's Cottage** and a second isolated cottage. Now stay on this track until reaching a bridge with a parking area beyond.

3 Do not cross the bridge, but turn sharp left here along another hard-surfaced track. Just before reaching a house, fork left on a path and when this soon ends at a T-junction, turn left along a wide bridleway. Along this track you will pass a couple of woodland pools where aquatic life will be seen. This bridleway brings us back to the junction of tracks by **Merritt's Cottage**.

To avoid heavy mud after prolonged rain during the depths of winter, turn right here and retrace your steps back to Hundred Pound Bridge car park from where we continue along Bookham Road to reach Downside and the end of this intriguing circuit.

4 At this junction of tracks by **Merritt's Cottage** turn right and after 25 yards fork left on a bridleway signed to **Effingham Common**. When this ends at a T-junction, turn right along a hard-surfaced path. After crossing a brook look out for a grassy path on your right 10 yards before reaching a junction of tracks with a house seen through the trees beyond. Now follow this grassy path that during winter can become quite sticky with mud, and soon after crossing a planked bridge you will meet up with **Hundred Pound Bridge** car park from where we continue along **Bookham Road** to reach **Downside** and the end of this intriguing circuit.

Places of interest nearby

Painshill Park in Cobham is said to be one of the 18th century's great landscape parks. It was the vision of a young nobleman, Charles Hamilton, who returned from Europe inspired by its art and architecture. The 'pleasure garden' contains a series of landscapes that delight the visitor. Follow the signs in Cobham. Open every day 10.30 am until dusk.
☎ *01932 584286*

11 Capel

The Crown Inn

Capel has long been bypassed by the A24 and is a pleasure to investigate, as is its church. This route leads us through farmed fields where the hedgerows are just brimming with birds and butterflies during summer. The turning point of the walk comes when we reach a large house named Temple Elfande which dates from 1541, although its foundations are far older as it once formed the centre of the manor that was given by John de Elfande to the Knights Templar from which it gets its name. The Templars originated in the 12th century and were a small band of fighting monks whose stated aim was 'to defend the Holy Sepulchre to the last drop of blood and fight the unfaithful wherever one finds them'. From here a quiet lane brings us to Aldhurst Farm where we re-cross fields to rejoin the village.

THE PUB

The **Crown Inn** can be dated back to 1687 and its closeness to the church of St John the Baptist has led to the theory that it once served as the vicarage. It was a hot day when I last visited and so I chose to forgo the lovely garden with its pond and fountain and sat in the coolness of the comfortable and welcoming bar. The reasonably priced menu offers plenty of choice from sandwiches, baguettes and light starters, to main courses that include a rib-eye steak dish with mushrooms, tomato and chips while from the pumps comes an ever changing selection of real ales.

Opening times: 12 noon to 2 pm and 4.30 pm to 11 pm weekdays, 11 am to 11 pm Saturdays and 12 noon to 10.30 pm on Sundays. Food is served each lunchtime and evening (not Sunday evening). Booking for evening meals is advisable.
☎ *01306 711130*

1 Walk along **Vicarage Lane**, which lies opposite the **Crown Inn** and when beside the entrance gates to a large Gothic house named **Charlotte Broadwood**, cross a stile to your right. Now

Distance – 3¾ miles.

OS Landranger 187 Dorking & Reigate, Crawley & Horsham. GR 176407.

An easy walk through level farmland.

Starting point The Crown Inn in the main village street.

How to get there *Capel is 5 miles south of Dorking and signed from the A24. There is plenty of parking alongside the main village street.*

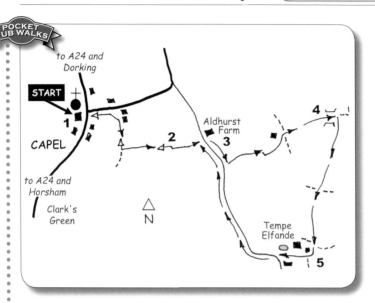

continue diagonally left across a meadow to the corner to meet the rear of stabling by a marker post. Turn right here and in a few yards cross a stile to enter a field where you continue along the right-hand edge to the top corner. Ignore a stile ahead of you and turn left along the top edge of the field.

2 At the corner of the field, go right over a stile and in 4 yards turn left on a path between young oak trees to reach another stile which you should cross. Go diagonally right over the meadow ahead and cross a stile in its corner and maintain direction on a waymarked path through woodland. After leaving the woodland, cross a small meadow towards the buildings of **Aldhurst Farm** to meet a quiet lane.

3 Turn right along the lane to meet with the entrance gates of an unseen house named **Temple Mead** to your left. Turn left here and after crossing two cattle grids continue along the concrete

Sixteenth-century Aldhurst Farm.

driveway. At a pair of rather more ornate gates to the house, go right through a field gate and turn left along the field edge. At the end of this field, cross a stile beside a field gate and follow the left edge of the next field. After passing through an avenue of oak trees, continue ahead through another field keeping a hedgerow close to your right.

4 At the end of this field, press on ahead on a raised track through a small wood to reach a farm bridge over a stream and a field

gate. Pass through the gate and turn right on a bridleway that continues along the right-hand side of three large fields. At the end of the third field ignore paths to left and right and go through a gate ahead and follow a path along a ribbon of woodland to soon reach a gate beside a brick building.

⑤ Ignore a bridleway to your left and continue ahead through the gate to meet a drive. Go ahead along the drive and pass **Temple Elfande** that disguises its age rather well under tile-hung walls. At the drive end, turn right along little-used **Temple Lane** where in ¾ mile you will meet with **Aldhurst Farm**. Turn left here over a stile and retrace your steps through a meadow and woodland before crossing a field diagonally right to a stile under a large oak tree. After passing between young oak trees seek out a half hidden stile on your right after which you should turn left along the field edge before going right to rejoin the stable buildings. Now turn left across a meadow to reach **Vicarage Lane** and the centre of the village.

Places of interest nearby

Horsham Cheese Shop, 20 Carfax, Horsham, sells fine British and Sussex cheeses and was nominated by the *Independent on Sunday* as the Best UK Cheese Shop and Delicatessen, while other credits include being featured by Rick Stein on BBC TV as one of his 'food heroes'. Handmade cheeses include Isle of Mull Cheddar, Colston Bassett, Stinking Bishop, Mature Wensleydale, Oxford Blue, Mature Lancashire, Blue Vinny, Olde Sussex, Goodwood Smoked, Somerset Brie and Smoked Lincolnshire Poacher.
☎ 01403 254272

The Running Horses

This marvellous walk begins in the village of Mickleham before following the course of the river Mole through the Mickleham Valley to meet the outskirts of Leatherhead where we pass through the grounds of Thorncroft Vineyard, makers of award-winning elderflower cordial. From here there is an easy climb to the rim of the valley that brings us to Bocketts Farm, a wonderland for children where you may well avail yourself of the splendid tearooms. The way continues along easy-to-follow tracks through the delights of Norbury Park where we pass Surrey Wildlife Trust's sawmill that makes anything from reserve signs to garden furniture from locally grown oak. From here the route makes an easy descent into the peaceful valley below and along the way you are treated to wonderful panoramic views across the vale.

Distance – 5¼ miles.

OS Landranger 187 Dorking & Reigate, Crawley & Horsham. GR 170535.

An easy walk that rises by a barely noticeable 220 feet before descending to the valley floor.

Starting point Old London Road, Mickleham.

How to get there Mickleham is on the B2209 Old London Road, 3 miles north of Dorking and just to the east of the A24. Parking at the roadside only.

THE PUB

The **Running Horses** gained its name from the Epsom Derby of 1828 which ended in a dead heat between two horses, *Cadland* and *The Colonel*. The race was later re-run and *Cadland* won. Both horses are featured on one face of the pub sign while *Cadland* hogs the reverse. I called in on a hot June lunchtime and the patio tables were already filling with visitors and so I sought the shade of the interior. The restaurant offers an extensive menu. I chose a simple tortilla – an omelette of potato, onion, cheese and herbs – from the bar menu where the dishes range from chunky sandwiches to salmon and crab fishcakes. From the pumps comes a good selection of draught ales that include Abbot Ale, Old Speckled Hen and Young's Best.

Opening times: 11.30 am to 11 pm each day (Sunday 12 noon to 10.30 pm). Booking a table in the restaurant for Friday, Saturday and Sunday is essential.
☎ *01372 372279*

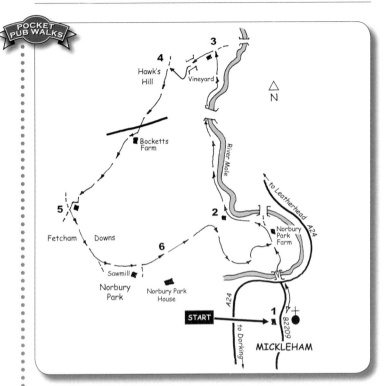

POCKET PUB WALKS

3

4
Hawk's Hill

Vineyard

△
N

River Mole

to Leatherhead A24

Bocketts Farm

5
Fetcham   Downs

2

Norbury Park Farm

6

Sawmill

Norbury Park

Norbury Park House

A24

START

to Dorking

1
B2209

MICKLEHAM

1 From the **Running Horses**, walk downhill to soon meet with the A24 dual carriageway. Here cross to the small bridge opposite that spans the **river Mole** and press on along a tarmac drive. At a fork in the drive, keep ahead and when a few yards past the ornate buildings of **Norbury Park Farm** – famous for its Norbury Blue cheese – fork left on a cart track between fields.

2 When the track ends beside **Lilac Cottage**, turn right on a wide track at the end of which pass through a gate. The way continues along the right side of a large meadow where you will see the **river Mole** below you. Pass through a gate at the end of this

meadow and keep ahead and soon go under a road bridge. Keep to the path as it soon skirts the **Thorncroft Vineyard** where you will see rows of elder trees from which they produce their award-winning elderflower cordial.

3 The path finally ends at a junction of tracks where you should turn left on a rising track that soon passes the vineyard buildings. Keep to the track after crossing a railway bridge and soon rejoin the vineyard. Here the path turns right and skirts the growing grounds before ending at a T-junction.

4 Turn left at this junction and continue along a bridleway that offers great views over the valley below. The bridleway ends at

A magnificent woodland clearing in Norbury Park.

a road, which you should cross to a track opposite that veers off rightwards and soon brings you to the entrance of **Bocketts Farm**, a superb children's farm that has a tearoom and garden that you can use without paying an entrance fee. The route continues ahead on a broad path between the farm entrance and a car park. Remain on this path and ignore paths into the woodland on your left.

5 A few yards after zigzagging around a field byre, turn left at a junction of tracks and follow a wide stony track through woodland. When a fork is met at the beginning of a large woodland clearing, keep to the left fork. Soon the track re-enters woodland and passes by a few picnic tables on the boundary of the **Surrey Wildlife Trust sawmill**. Here the way meets with a tarmac driveway and you should continue ahead to pass the gates of **Norbury Park House**.

6 Your climb to these heights is now rewarded with an easy descent along this pleasant driveway that eventually leaves the woodland and continues between open fields where there are great views over the vale. Remain on the drive until it meets with another at the foot of the hill where you should turn right and retrace your steps back to **Mickleham** and the end of this great circuit.

Places of interest nearby

Bocketts Farm, 1 mile south-west of Leatherhead off the A246, is a working family farm with old and modern breeds of animals plus other attractions that will interest adults as well as their main audience of children. Depending on the time of year there is a chance to see sheep shearing and haymaking plus the births of lambs, piglets, ducklings and goslings. Open every day (except Christmas and New Year's Day) from 10 am to 6 pm or dusk if earlier.
☎ *01372 363764*

13 Outwood

The Bell Inn

This superb circuit is one of the best field walks** that I know of in Surrey. After leaving Outwood Common and its ancient working windmill, we walk a charming byway southwards that is now only used by those on foot or horseback before turning east and following field paths towards the steeple of Horne church. A short section of country lane follows before the route heads north across rising fields where magnificent views across the Surrey and Kent Weald are to be had. The shorter circuit now heads back to Outwood while the longer route follows a lovely cart track with panoramic views and passes Lodge Farm before following more cart tracks through magnificent countryside. After crossing a country lane, the circuit continues through the scenic fields of Burstow Park Farm where glorious field paths return us to Outwood Common and the end of this great circuit.

THE PUB The **Bell Inn** is just 100 yards north of the windmill in Outwood Lane and makes the perfect spot to sit and relax after a good walk. A riot of beams believed to have come from a Charles II man-o'-war welcomes you in the bar and restaurant while the garden that overlooks the countryside is

Distance – 3 or 6 miles.

OS Landranger 187 Dorking & Reigate, Crawley & Horsham. GR 327456.

An easy walk through undulating countryside.

Starting point National Trust free car park on Outwood Common.

How to get there Outwood is 3 miles south of Bletchingley which sits astride the A25. Turn into Outwood Lane opposite Bletchingley's church and continue until the windmill is reached. Turn right opposite the mill on a dirt track that leads to the small car park.

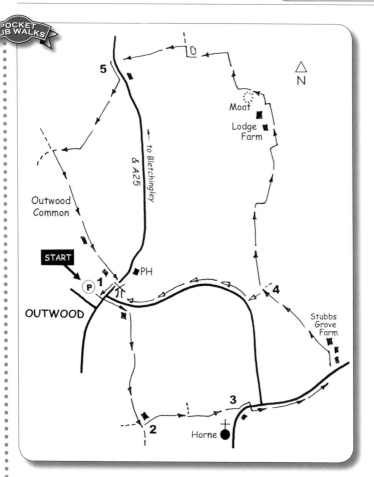

a real treat during the summer. The food ranges from simple bar snacks and daily specials to a more formal dish of braised lamb shank served with three-bean cassoulet and mustard mashed potato. The beers from the pumps include Harvey's Best bitter and Spitfire as well as the usual lagers.

Opening times: 11 am to 11 pm each day (Sunday 12 noon to 10.30 pm). Food is served lunchtimes and evenings and booking for the restaurant is required on busy summer weekends.
☎ *01342 842989*

[1] From the parking area, walk back to the road and press on ahead along **Gayhouse Lane** and pass the windmill. Turn right on a public byway beside a cottage named **Knowle Green** and follow this ancient track gently downhill to meet a tarmac drive by a house named **Wilmot's Farm**. Pass the house and at the end of its garden, turn left on a signed footpath.

[2] Turn left at a field edge and continue along its left side to meet its corner. Press on through a second field keeping a hedgerow on your left and at a third field go directly across its centre towards a gap in the hedgerow under an oak tree. Again maintain direction, this time with a hedge and ditch close to your right. Follow the field edge leftwards to a marker post and turn right. Follow the right side of a field until it opens up and then go ahead aiming to the left of a house and pass through a gate.

[3] Continue alongside a hedgerow with a lane beyond and pass through a kissing gate on your right to meet the lane. Turn left along the lane and remain on it until a group of houses are met. Turn left on a drive leading to **Stubbs Grove Farm** and near the drive end turn left on a signed path that skirts a paddock. Cross a brook and enter a field where you follow an indistinct path ahead and slightly leftwards. Pass through a hedgerow and turn left for 5 yards before turning right and crossing a meadow diagonally left to its top left corner. Pass through a line of trees and maintain direction ahead over a meadow towards woodland.

Outwood's famous old mill.

4 Enter woodland to meet a wide crossing track in 20 yards.

It is here that the shorter circuit continues by turning left along the track to soon meet Gayhouse Lane. Turn right and follow the lane back to Outwood Common.

The longer route continues ahead on a wonderful track alongside fields and brings us to **Lodge Farm**. About 80 yards before the farm buildings, turn right on a path that brings you to the concrete farm drive. Turn left through the farm gate and then right in 5 yards on a wonderful cart track that now zigzags alongside fields. When the edge of woodland is met on your left, turn left alongside it to meet a cart track and a lane beyond.

5 With caution, cross the road and turn left along it for a short distance before turning right through a kissing gate opposite a cottage by the **Outwood Swan Sanctuary**. The path now crosses three rising fields diagonally leftwards. At the top corner of the third field turn right along a field edge to meet a stile under an oak tree in 50 yards. Turn left over the stile and continue with a hedgerow on your left. At the field end, cross a meadow and pass through a line of trees to join a drive by some cottages. Follow the drive to meet **Outwood Common** where the **Bell Inn** will be found ahead on the left while the parking area is to your right.

Places of interest nearby

Outwood windmill is the oldest working windmill in Britain although nowadays it only produces small quantities of flour for visitors. Open on summer Sundays and Bank Holidays between 2 pm and 6 pm (www.outwoodwindmill.co.uk).

14 Warlingham

The White Lion

This surprisingly rural circuit lies only one mile outside the border of the London Borough of Croydon and begins in the centre of Warlingham where it takes only a few yards to leave the hustle and bustle of the village behind. We follow footpaths and bridleways that lead us easily towards a lovely coppice to the south of Chelsham where the route soon meets and follows for a short distance the Vanguard Way long-distance path. As we begin to head back towards Warlingham, the walk passes a pool on Chelsham Common where a couple of seats entice you to take time out and watch dragonflies hunting above the water in summer. Continuing along the long-distance path a little further brings us to a bridleway that offers rural views as well as returning us to Warlingham where we retrace our steps to the centre of the village.

THE PUB

The **White Lion** started life as a farmhouse and the middle section, which is clearly the oldest, is believed to date from 1467. Duck as you walk through the door as there are low beams galore and a warren of small intimate bar areas that are a pleasure to explore – from the lovely snug of yesteryear to the larger contemporary bar and restaurant areas at the back that fit in surprisingly well. The menu offers dishes that range from a mushroom and stilton melt to vegetable tagine with grilled Scottish salmon and all at very reasonable prices. From the pumps come real ales such as Bombardier, Pedigree, Young's and London Pride.

Opening times: 12 noon to 11 pm each day. Food is served throughout the day until 9 pm.
☎ *01883 629011*

[1] When facing the **White Lion**, go right along **Farleigh Road** and pass the **Horseshoe pub**. Turn left into **Mint Walk** and at its end

Distance – 3¾ miles.

OS Landranger 187 Dorking & Reigate, Crawley & Horsham. GR 356585

An easy walk through fairly level countryside.

Starting point The White Lion in Farleigh Road. Plenty of roadside parking will be found in Farleigh Road.

How to get there Warlingham is 5 miles south of Croydon town centre on the B269 Limpsfield Road. Farleigh Road and the White Lion are a few yards south of the small one-way system in the centre of the village.

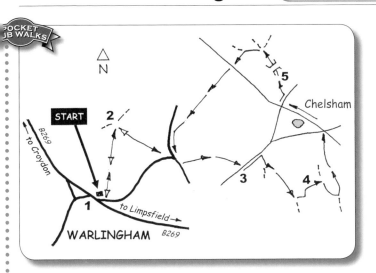

go ahead on a signed footpath that passes a children's play area. Ignore side paths and continue alongside a field and through woodland to meet a kissing gate. Go through the gate and keep ahead across a small meadow and pass through another kissing gate to join a junction of tracks.

2 Turn sharp right here and follow a stony bridleway downhill until it ends at a road and turn left to meet a road junction by a mini-roundabout. Turn right at the roundabout and in 60 yards turn left on a bridleway along **Greenhill Lane**. When the road soon ends go ahead between posts and continue along the bridleway as it passes between fields.

3 The bridleway ends at a road and you should turn left along the pavement. A few yards before an entrance gate on your right, turn right on a bridleway. At the end of a garden to your left, turn left on a footpath that skirts the garden and brings you to a field edge. Keep to the path as it follows the field edge before continuing through oak woodland. At a small junction of paths by

A wildlife pond along the route.

a directional post with a field end to your left, turn left ignoring a stile on your immediate left. At a grassy T-junction with a field to your right, turn left to soon meet a junction of tracks under a large beech tree.

4 Turn right here and follow the fenced path through marvellous woodland until it ends at a T-junction with a stony track. The track forms a part of the **Vanguard Way** long-distance footpath and you should now turn left along it. The track ends at a road junction where you should go ahead along **Ledgers Road**. Along the road you will see a pond to your left and a couple of inviting seats. Turn right at a road junction and after 100 yards turn left on a signed footpath, again a part of the **Vanguard Way**.

5 After passing the manicured grounds of what was once **Warlingham Park Hospital**, pass under a small bridge and press on to meet with a junction of tracks. Turn left here along a bridleway and when the end of a road is met, bear left along it to reach a road junction. Go ahead on a bridleway opposite until it ends at another road. Now turn left downhill to reach the mini-roundabout passed earlier. Turn right here and a few yards later, right again along the bridleway where you now retrace your steps back to the centre of **Warlingham** and the end of this circuit.

Places of interest nearby

Titsey Place is a hidden gem set in 18 acres of restored gardens that surround the historic mansion. As well as the mansion, there are greenhouses displaying exotic plants, an organic kitchen garden and picnic area. Titsey is off the B269, 4 miles south of Warlingham. Open from mid May to the end of September on Wednesdays, Sundays and Bank Holidays from 1 pm until 5 pm.
☎ *01273 407056*

The Royal Oak

Although Staffhurst Wood is famous for its springtime display of bluebells, it is well worth a visit at any time of year. This short, but lovely walk remains within the woodland for almost its entire route and is particularly good on a hot summer's day when the cool shade that the trees offer is sought. It is believed that this remnant of ancient woodland, an SSSI, has existed since at least Saxon times and was once a royal hunting forest. Even today, commoners retain their rights on parts of it. After crossing a meadow behind the pub we reach the woodland where we follow wide paths beneath tall oak and beech trees. Never far from roads, the route weaves its way through the magnificent forest before reaching the tiny hamlet of Merle Common from where it is but a short stroll back to the Royal Oak.

Distance – 2¼ miles.

OS Landranger 187 Dorking & Reigate, Crawley & Horsham. GR *pub 407485, St Silvan's car park 410488.*

An easy walk through gently undulating countryside.

Starting point The Royal Oak car park (please ask first) or at point 3, St Silvan's car park, Staffhurst Wood.

How to get there *Staffhurst Wood is 3 miles south of the A25 at Limpsfield.*

THE PUB The **Royal Oak** is a friendly pub known to regulars as 'Churchill's local' due to its proximity to Chartwell. The owners are rightly proud of their home-cooked food; the bar menu offers a selection that includes open sandwiches and ploughman's lunches while from the à la carte menu is a tempting dish of belly of pork with honey-roasted vegetables. Plenty of real ales supplement the good food and being a traditional country pub, dogs are just as welcome in the bar as their owners.

Opening times: 11 am to 11 pm each day (Sunday 12 noon until 10 pm). Food served lunchtimes and evenings with a 'happy hour' menu Monday to Friday between 6 pm and 7 pm. Booking is required at all times for cooked meals.
☎ *01883 722207*

1 When facing the pub, turn right and in 60 yards cross a stile on your left. Follow the left side of the field and cross a stile in the top left corner. Now continue ahead through the next field and pass through a small gate 20 yards to the left of a field

Surrey

gate ahead of you. Go along the edge of a small meadow and after passing through a second gate follow the path rightwards to meet with a road. Go diagonally right over the road to a signed footpath and follow this as it enters woodland. Ignore paths to left and right and continue to a T-junction with a meadow seen through the trees ahead.

2 Turn left here and in 20 yards pass a small woodland pool. After a further 20 yards, by a junction of paths and a post, turn left on a narrower path. After climbing a rise the path levels to meet with a junction of tracks by a post. Go ahead and pass through a wooden barrier and after passing through a second barrier fork rightwards to soon meet a road and enter **St Silvan's car park** opposite.

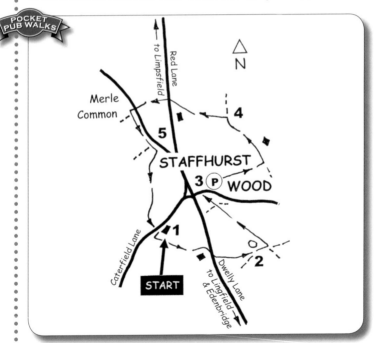

A wide track through the forest.

3 From the car park, go between wooden posts and follow the wide path that is furthest away from the entrance. Remain on the main path as it goes gently downhill between trees before ending at a barrier with a T-junction and a tarmac path beyond. Turn left along the hard-surfaced path and within yards pass by a concrete water reservoir. The path and reservoir are reminders that during the Second World War this area was an ammunition dump run by Canadians. *It is important now that the following directions are not missed.* Remain on this wide path when it bends right and ignore a directional post and path on your left. At a second right bend ignore a crossing path in 20 yards. After going down a slope, another crossing path is met and it is here that you should leave the track by turning left.

4 The path now continues within the wood and remains parallel with the edge of a field seen through the trees on your right. After climbing a rise, the path ends at a sharp left turn by a gate. Turn right here and cross a stile. Go diagonally left through a corner of a field to reach and cross a stile beside an electricity substation. Go over a lane and continue on the signed path opposite. When the path is joined by another from the left, go ahead to meet a fork in 5 yards and follow the left fork. Soon bear left at a garden fence and continue to meet a road in the hamlet of **Merle Common**. Turn left alongside the road and ignore a signed footpath on your right between houses in 90 yards. Continue along the road and pass **Merle Common House**.

5 After climbing a rise in the road and passing two further houses, a couple of signed footpaths are met on your right. Ignore the first path but follow the second as it forks right away from the road and follows an ancient bank through majestic woodland. When the bank turns right by 90 degrees, bear right to soon meet a wide crossing track. Continue ahead here over a small plank bridge and between posts. Pass a **Woodland Trust** welcome sign and follow the well-trodden path as it passes a corner of a field and over another plank bridge. Continue ahead when a path joins from the left and in 30 yards go ahead at a crossing track by a seat. Within yards of passing an information board, a road and the **Royal Oak** are met. *If you began the walk at St Silvan's car park continue with points 1 and 2.*

Places of interest nearby

Chartwell, located 2 miles south of Westerham off the B2026, was home to Sir Winston Churchill and is now a National Trust property. The kitchen garden incorporates the Golden Rose Avenue created by Sir Winston's children in 1958 to celebrate their parents' golden wedding anniversary. Open from mid March until the end of October, Wednesday to Sunday (plus Tuesday in mid summer).
☎ *01732 868381*